harvest

Harvest
by Elodie Parthenay

Illustration & Cover Design by Julie Solvstrom

if you're feeling like you've gotten lost
on the road to radical joy,
help is on the way.

contents

sunburst

The road to joy
was never a detour,
skirting around
the waves of my heart
or the weather in my mind—
every twist and turn
drove me right through them.

I am not
who I was a year ago,

I am even more
of myself.

The sun finds me sweetened and ripe,
oranges on an altar.

For a year I trailed
a road dotted with cardinals
fist clenched, looking away
    they flew back threefold.

Until I woke up to a tree flapping with red wings

Until I opened the gift of surrender and made it my own

Until I showed blind faith to the road
and to the guides' knowledge

to the dreams and the synchronicities
to the soft heart tissue swelling
to the chambers bursting with joy;
magic.

This road of birds led me back to
your flesh   our connection
portal
for divine longing

Since then, each dawn has found me
in bed with my self
full of some
thing

only felt.

Standing
straight—

not leaning on you.
Not chasing,
not running away.

Standing tall,

    sunflower.

Palms up,
open hands—

not clinging.
Not keeping
you tightly trapped in.

Receiving

what's meant to be mine,
celebrating what wants to stay.

As I evolved,
I didn't expect
my dreams

to expand
grow wider
more ambitious
take up more space

Never dreamed
I could dream
so big

With a whole lot of patience
and a whole lot of softness,
things are slowly falling back
into place.

When I felt like I couldn't walk anymore
I crawled
and sat among the flowers
right in the sun
their leaves a shield
Among them I remembered
joy was inside me all along
available to be picked
like a ripe fruit—
I bit inside its soft flesh
let its juices quench my thirst
run sweet rivers along my lips
pollinize my soul
flower inside me

I am learning
that I don't have to be
in control at all times and
that I don't always have
to know what I'm doing

I'm leaning
a little more towards chaos
and surrender these days,
and maybe I don't have
to always be a good person

What I'm saying is
that if I can't find what feels right,
maybe a valid alternative to stillness
is to do what feels good
right now.

Your body
and mine,
our conversations,
how we're working
at communicating better,
that reciprocity,
how safe I feel and
how you say I'm easy to talk to—
that is the poetry.
Words are only a vessel.

Hours roll away like waves
and we're still breathing underwater
You say time is the only thing leaving—
lover, it never applied to us
Not the days or the milestones
What we share is infinite.

You, darling, were the spark—
when the light dims, I think about you
and feel the core reignite.

Let's be so full of joy,
so full of honesty
and pure love
that fear has no place to grow

Thank you for reminding me how it feels to be safe
Thank you for lighting up a raging fire in my belly

Thank you for tending to my heart garden
after the floods and the calamities

You were a season, a spring or a summer
of growth and healing, of joy and finding
the way to myself again—

Thank you for drenching it with glorious sun,
Thank you for paving every step with wildflowers.

Part the halves
of my heart and sigh
as you sink between them—
Don't move, don't go anywhere,
All we desire is right here

I came here looking
for radiant joy—
you gave me soft smiles,
gentle understanding,
but mostly, you held me
in your arms when upset washed over me.
Instead of joy, darling,
you gave me peace.
That wasn't what I was seeking.
That is invaluable.

The greatest gift
your love gives me
is the ease
that comes with the absence
of uncertainty.

I can't say I missed you
because there was never a gap to be filled.
I won't say you make me happy—
I already was before you came.

What you do is bring depth
of perception
like a kaleidoscope

through you
every parcel of joy in my life
appears multiplied
simply by way of you
existing

Watered by your hand,
I see sides of myself
I'd never met before—this one bites
into the pink flesh of oranges,
that one keeps red apples on the counter,
one folds herself around your body at night,
while another grows roots out of cut flowers,
turns something that wasn't meant to last
into lasting, blooming life.

I don't need to know
what will happen next—

I'm plenty satisfied

knowing we're both feeling
out our way through the dark

together.

Bite into me
like you do those Florida oranges
I miss the sun
and the warmth of your palms
I long to see
those gold tones of yours
as I taste salt on your skin
sticky sweet   sunkissed
from the life you had before we met.
Darling I've never waited
so hard for summer to come.

When fear wakes me,
seeping into my dreams,
you're here.

If tomorrow the sun rises
on our celestial bodies—

let me enjoy our day for
what it is

instead of beating us up
for everything we can't be.

Can we enjoy this moment,
taste it fully, with all its luscious flavors,
roll it on our tongues and take
deep whiffs off each other?

The electric touch
of your fingers grazing my palm
and the way my stomach churns when
your eyes meet my skin—
that is the only knowledge I seek.

That certainty is enough for now.

I am done
running
or chasing—
a woman gets tired.

These days I just want to

live well.

not postpone joy
as a prize to be earned, but
find it now,
find it here,

open my windows wide
and claim it as mine,

feel
it
        coursing and sparking in my cells,
myself opening up
        like a sun-drenched blossom,

and stand very still, in this very moment,
to enjoy its taste fully
on the tip of my soul.

You say I do to you
like the moon does the tides
Darling, a bond like ours
would make anyone spiritual

Darling, I still hold space
for your mind and heart.

Relationships will fade, evolve,
and what are we left with, if not
someone's hand in ours?

I only hope
I left you   overflowing with love and light,

I only hope
I left you   better than I found you.

　　　　—taurus venus

It's the way you hold on to me in your sleep,
like you're afraid I might go,
like I might be a dream.

Falling for you was like slipping
into the ocean, unaware
of its depth and mysteries

Lover, once I dived
there was no returning
to solid ground.

Give me your fingers, darling

Slide
them in the spaces
between mine

Put them
in my mouth

Run

them through my hair
hold tight—

Don't let go.

I started setting the table
for you years ago.

Hunger strikes,
wet jaw gaping at

the poetic rhythm of you,
flesh inside my mouth—intricate dance

The desperate longing to have you
be a part of me, never apart

Halving, sharing,
symbiotic organism.

Even when you're not around
I feel held

All there is ahead of us
is time
and blue skies, baby.

How lucky are we—
we're both the lucky ones

Where my solar warmth
meets your ocean blues
is where forever lies,
cosmic connection.

Sometimes your face pops into my mind
like a stolen transmission
and I can't help but smile—

sometimes laugh.

It's a joke only me
and the Universe are privy to.

Many came before you—
everybody loves a hot spot
Excitement wears off
and fear does too, sometimes

But lover, you're a local now
Coasts known by heart
under the palm of your hand
And still, here is where you rush
as dawn rises and
the downtown bells ring
with unwavering worship

They were there all along,
hidden
in little moments that felt just right,
once I discovered how to pause,
explore and expand them—

the peace that comes with
alignment and knowing
that right here is where I belong
and what I was meant to experience—

that joy blooming,
filling my body
up to the brim,
spilling over.

Only when I can taste the fear
do I live this loud,
only when I can taste the fear
is my tongue this sharp.

I never realized
how vulnerable I was
until you showed me
what it feels like
to be safe.

It's not enough
for my mind to tell me it makes sense
and it's not enough
for my heart to tell me I like them—

what matters is
the soul
what matters
is on a cellular level
what matters is
if my soul vibrates with joy
from the way we connect together

You come back home
with the first winter snow,
hands full—
oranges and pomegranates
and fresh flowers in sunshine shades

My heart is
a blossoming spring—
early blooms of adoration,
the dawn of something
infinite.

When you know, you know, they say
and when I met you I knew

that up until that moment
I hadn't known a thing at all.

Joy as a practice
joy as a commitment
joy as a revolutionary act
joy as a beacon
joy as a natural resource
to share and to build a house around.

blossoms

For so long I held on tight
to the familiar and the lost

but as I stare into the void—
infinite unborn possibilities—

slowly unclenching my fingers,
taking a grounding breath,

I realize,

liberation starts with
letting go.

Where I'm going,
I can't afford to keep
pocketfuls of past
weighing me down.

I stumbled upon joy in
a happy accident:
first I met you—a hard fall
that propelled me towards
everything that made me feel alive
in a bid to fill the hungry void you left
with other living, beating things.

Stepping outside.

Showing up.

Hands shaking, but
walking still. Sitting down. Staying.

Regaining territory.
Better yet, expanding.

I let you water my garden for a while,
but I was blooming before you came
and I'll bloom long after you're gone.

As easier as it would be to hate you
you moved me to greatness
I can't separate joy from you.

None of my trees bore fruit
this year. They bloomed beautifully,
wrapped in petal promises
of abundance. I sit in yellow grass,
admiring the crooked shelter
I built with my broken body
and all the things I learned,
all the things I did despite it all,
all the things I'll build on
when the sun comes back.
The cardinals are gone
and new birds will take their place
sooner or later—I know that
for sure now.

With each step I take,
raw soles on burning soil,
I realize I didn't need to
wait to be healed
to move on.

I confused
the butterflies in my stomach
for love once
when they were just
          anxiety

so whenever I feel them now
I always think I'm anxious
when the truth is
I am excited—

excited to see how I'll grow next.

Big knife
cutting satisfying slices—

zucchinis and carrots
and healing ginger.

The yellow pepper in the bottom drawer
has softened gray— will you even notice
that this too is missing?

I can't fix everything, but the red curry
and the maple syrup–sweetened gesture,
they'll honey out the cracks in your throat
and maybe the soft holes in your heart.

I drove over and left
the warm jar at your door—
not as an apology or a consolation prize,
but as proof

that I am here. Still.
        Call me.

I don't miss you
as I would a long lost limb,
      I hunger.
The sight of you fuels me,
leaves me
           full and satisfied.

Your presence
is a precious resource.
Your presence
is a gift.

I don't regret falling,
or the way I rolled up to your feet,
ripe for the picking. Do you know
how hard I worked
to give in to trust?

Your open hand closed into a fist,
you couldn't bear that sweetness—you,
still green, yet hardened; weathered
by years of biting cold,
and relentless abuse.

You took a bite
but you'd sooner let yourself starve
than risk running out of that taste—
Better run now, and forget it!

Me, I will be fine,
I'll sprout new roots, I'll grow again—
what's one more little bruise?
Watch my body, bent and broken,
I'm blooming already!

Darling, I wanted you
so hard
to be the destination

but I'm so grateful
for you
were and continue to be
the way.

Tonight I stand on the precipice
of accepting
that I wasn't made for normalcy,
for basic

Gratefulness rushes,
sweet anticipation of
not sweating to contort simple shapes
into sophisticated holes

I let what doesn't fit fall and
instead of grief
I feel relieved—
    release

Tonight I stand on the precipice
of accepting
that my options may be few,
but they are worth so much more.

If you're not here to love me right
don't crowd my space
If you're not here to love me right
why did you come at all?

How do you carry
the unspoken expectation that
this fire is meant to be
fleeting

when you are wired
for forever?

I used to fear
not you, but myself around you—
in these strange times, I feared
          everything. Especially
a good thing.

But today, I'm going to
kiss you
          instead of waiting, hopeful,
          for you to make that move
tell you all the things, all the
          silly things
          that go through my mind
sit on your lap
          and press my body into yours
wrap you whole in my arms
          whenever I feel like it

and then I'll leave,
when I feel ready to.

Today
might be the day

maybe
we're getting it right
this time.

Your warmth,

it made me ripe,
it made me sweet.

I stared up towards you,
stretching myself taller,
watched you go,
            and waited
for you to come back

and when you didn't,
as stars do sometimes,
I looked at my reflection,
and found all the light I needed.

            —heliotropism

For so long I wondered
if you could want me too,
now my main concern is:
can you love me right?

The moon rises
in Cancer and awakens
past misses
and missed loves

It's not today I'm weeping for

but for the version of me I used to be,
how heartache tore my chest
and how powerless I felt

for what withered before it could bloom
for what was never born

The moon has me
looking backward and inward
and as a new lunation dawns in the morning,
I'll be walking forward

healed.

embracing the unknown
embracing the discomfort
of not knowing
of not being in control

surrendering

as I let go of the cliff
as the wall comes hurtling faster

softening

instead of tightening myself
into anxious knots

letting it happen
letting it happen and smiling

actively surrendering
not jumping but falling

into what's supposed to be
into what's best for me
into joy and out of fear, and above all
more in love with myself with
every waking moment

Always astounds me
how some people love standing
under my window, calling out my name,
only to take off running
the second I open the door.

The thing with letting go
of the weight of
my own expectations
is that I will rise,
no matter the outcome.

Some fall in love
with people's potential—

I see myself in strangers
and fall in love
with who I could be.

Had I been sleeping for
the hundreds of seasons before
I gazed into your mirror eyes
and saw the universe in me
birthed to life, moons and suns—

seasons of pleasure and joy
and sweet longing
spent trapped, locked in
dim-lighted ignorance
with only a speckle of
awareness of my own highness,
and exquisite reality—

what I mean darling,
is that in meeting you,
I met myself.

I am done with crumbs.
From now on,
I am not sitting down
for anything less than a feast.

I don't miss
what could have been—
I'm far away now
from who I used to be.

Love and softness
for Brown and Black women
and the freedom to be wholly our selves

I am not a wild animal,
a curved vessel for the world's fantasies
or three stereotypes in a trench coat.

  —wishes

I wanted to send you
some Fairmount bagels
but I didn't know
when you'd be home—
it might be news to you, darling,
but some things get stale
when left unattended.

What scared me most
was the risk of losing you,

and now that I have
there's nothing left for me

     to fear.

I used to be so thankful
that you came into my life right
when I needed it—you beautiful
oblivious idiot—

you had no idea
what you were doing,
how could you have known
the power you were awaking?

Sunset came
and a new day arrived
and with the morning, came enlightenment—

the universe knew exactly
what I needed
and how to wrap it
to make sure I wouldn't miss the delivery.

Gone are the days
of confusing
peaches for oranges
and attraction or familiarity
for celestial signs

When I say I left
because you couldn't commit,

I didn't mean
white dress, champagne and rings plucked
from my favorite shop in Brooklyn—

it was never about a do-over.

What I wanted, love, was
an eclipse
       of your intentions and your actions:
       Aligned. Powerful.
you,
       running towards your desires
       and daring them to come your way,
       sowing poppies and sunflowers in your garden
       just so you could pick them up for me next season

It was never about the chase—

what I wanted, love
was a harvest.

Is this the warmth
I convinced myself
I didn't need?

After the eclipses and the escapes,
I trailed for weeks
only to find that feeling lost
isn't a curse, for you get the luxury
to find yourself again.

Getting to start again feels like
falling in reverse, upward
into the night sky —
so many possibilities,
no way to tell where I'm going,
and my stomach too is unsettled
but the view's going to be amazing,
and the story will be worth it.

This garden
will flower again next year

and so will I.

And when we meet again
and you ask me where I've been

 deep in my own head
 right in my own way

I hope by then I've learned
to be elsewhere entirely

 in the moment
 submerged in joy

echo

What's left between us
is distance
of geography and heart,
and missed coordinates—
be them of space or time.
But I had to walk that mile, lover.
I had to make you past.

I have tried to be reasonable about us
but darling,
reason deserted this place
a long time ago.

You touch me as soon as I come in
and I taste it
warm on my tongue, bitter—
unfulfilled desire

just like a year ago

maybe one day
I squash it down,
the sudden wave of wanting,
maybe one day
I bite my tongue
for as long as I'm around

my fist tightens around our memories
and I linger longer than I should

I want to stay here, inside of you
it's unbearable to leave
never to have you completely.

—Tkaronto

Love looks like the black
lines on your back,
my first morning sight
on the good days,
my last memory on the others—
my last memory on most.

It is the amber scent
of you—patchouli and amber—
it's tattooed on my clothes,
it clouds the rooms you
didn't follow me in
and my car on the drive back.

You changed fragrances since I met you,
you changed cities
and you changed
lovers
but love has stayed still
fossilized
        eroding.

We get lost
in translation
or maybe it's dimensions

I give you space
when what you need is time

I'm unsure how to navigate
this—can we share coordinates?

We never said it was love,
but looking back,
it could have been—

fear has a way
of fucking up a beautiful thing.

Have you ever known
in the most certain part of your mind
that something was over and yet

felt your body get up in arms
and your heart grow
armor against that fact?

There's no rationalizing
waves of sensations and feelings—
that tide keeps on coming.

Just like traumatic memories
pull you back into the past,
exquisite ones
have a way of seeping into the now.

I was afraid you might be
not just gone, but dead

and here you were,

dying

a thousand little deaths
over a stranger's body.

When you come to mind,
I feel no anger.

It must be terrible to be so afraid
of what you desire most
that you'd rather deprive yourself of it
than ever risk losing it.

When you come to mind,
I feel no anger—only a bit
of sadness sprinkled
with nostalgia, and the urge
to hug the little kid inside you,
knowing I can't fix you,
only walk away.

Exhaustion combusts my spirit
Needles pierce my lungs
I'm tired   of running
of trying to catch up for
years underwater
years unlived

I kiss with the urgency
of someone who knows lightning
lights the sky for a second only,
bereavement of the heart
is impending
and good things,
they can drop dead any second.

I am aware I am throwing
my insecurities
at the walls you built up
and seeing what sticks.

Long after you were gone
I still sought your silhouette of mist
on street corners we kissed

Long after you were gone
Long after I swore I was done
I still sought your features
in the faces of new lovers

But there's no one like you, honey
memories lack and my dreams too
Chaos, wit and silver rings
You strange, beautiful thing
there's no conjuring you
out of thin air, out of the blue

There's not a thing like you.

There's not enough aliveness in me just yet
to birth a new self
Let me stay stuck a while.

Some songs will always make me rain—
unannounced turbulent weather
off the familiar coasts of
your face and your departure,
the relief of your hands,
the peaks of that laugh of yours
in my memories.
The storm rolls out—
blinding clouds on my foggy face
My heart thunders, I burst
in deafening light

       and it passes,
love, it passes. But
some songs will always
make me rain.

Nothing haunts you like
the ghost of what could have been

the one who didn't announce it was leaving
or tell you why.

If we meet again,

let it be a ray of light
instead of a long-awaited breath.

Let me feel joy
instead of relief.

What I mean is—
while I hope I do see you again
I don't want to forget
myself in the meantime, or
wait in the sidelines, disconnected.

At the end of the day, I owe
loyalty to myself.

I miss
the idea of you,
the form that took shape
in the negative space
between the things you didn't do
and the ones you showed you could,
between the words I didn't expect
and the ones that hung unsaid.

I reach for it;
an extended hand based
on a yearlong of hopes—

nothingness.
A past long gone,
a truth that never really was.

They say fear is birthed from the unknown.
For me, it jumps right
out of familiar outcomes.

I know you're afraid
of us
but I am not.

I told you,
I love an adventure.

elodie parthenay

I lean into you like an aching branch
extending towards the sun
fruits ripe and heavy
with sugar and wanting

Your caress, a ray of light
goldens my skin,
snakes through raised bumps—
everything falls down,
sinks,
like teeth

Sweet vertigo.

You say *this is nice,*
somehow that's enough.

I say *this is nice*
and I want this all the time, forever—

how can there ever be enough
of such a good thing?

I dreaded heartbreak
but less than I dreaded you.
Fell asleep in your collar
and the awareness we were through,
woke up to your back—
oh the lucky hands who drew
the landscapes and the faces—
I wonder if you knew
how much worry weighed on me
what if we don't make it—god, what if we do?

I've long wondered why
I still slip so easy
into writing about you, into
thinking about us

Truth is,
romancing reality is trickier
than longing
for what never was.

Is it something I did
or is it something
I am

I just need to know
what part of me
you are rejecting

—the intersectionality of not fitting in

It's only now dawning on me
that I've walked through deserts
for as long as I remember,
hoping to find my way back home.

circle

The universe working its magic
doesn't always manifest as
signs and synchronicities—

sometimes it's a rug
pulled from right under your feet.

Can we try to own our shit
be vulnerable
and communicate
from a place of honesty?

What is that bitterness, and where does it come from?
What gave birth to it, what part of yourself did it hatch in before
poisoning your veins as it traveled to your lips?

Take a shovel, lover, and dig.

Here's the core, grab it—Are you afraid?
Here's the root, pull it—Is it love?

Shake the dirt off, study it.

Only if you get your hands dirty,
only if you do the back-breaking work
can our garden grow.

The most important thing
I've learned this year
is to stop looking outside of myself
for a fix to what is happening
on the inside.

You've fought enough, darling.
You've held on tight enough to
what you desired, what was resisting.

Unclench that fist,
try an open palm for a while.
Stand back a little straighter—notice
how you've been bending

Now's the time to surrender.
Now's your time
to flower.

If you enter love, enter it fully—
don't cheat yourself by not showing up,
don't deprive yourself
of the warmth intimacy brings
by staying in the doorway, in the drafts.

If you're simultaneously pushing the gas pedal
and slamming on the brakes,
do you think you'll go anywhere?

May you get to make
the wonderful discovery
of who you are when
you are loved right.

Even if you're one of those
soft, caring souls
who are always ready
to share what they own,

—especially,
if you are one of those
willing to half their needs
to fill somebody else's void—

remember:
it's okay for you to have it all.

Take all the space.
Feel all the joy.
Have all the success.
Just because it's not shared
doesn't mean it's worth less.

Shut out
all the outside noise
every now and then,
focus only on your own
beautiful cacophony.

You can build bridges
over the trenches
that separate you from them.

You can open your heart home
like a warm hotel lobby
and take their baggage along.

You can be a garden
full of ripe fruits
ready for them to feast on.

And you can let your gentle soul
grow tired
or bitter with disappointment.

Or you can meet them right
where they are, and see
if that's a place you'd like
to stay for a while.

There is magic
in knowing in your heart
that this is not your fault,
and their behavior is not reflective
of your value or lack thereof—
a healing spell, right there.

If you've been raised to notice
people's subtle cues
as a safety measure,

here's a lesson
you'd better learn
sooner than later:

there are no awards
for accurately guessing
what drives people
to act the way they do.

You will have to forgive yourself
for all those times you forgot yourself.

Can you believe
you deserve
what you're running towards?

The hardest thing about getting back out there
after mending your shattered heart
is pretending it never happened
whenever you feel those cracks
threatening to open again.

The hardest thing is being fearless
through the piercing awareness
of the worst that could happen.

The hardest thing is not letting fear
mold someone new
into the shape of someone gone.

The only way to bring out of others
what a good lover
has brought out of you
is to be completely,
unapologetically, and fearlessly
yourself.

Every once on a while, if you're lucky,
you'll get to meet someone—
not as a human, but as a soul

by which I mean
you'll recognize each other,
          instant connection
talk about your strange habits,
your weird childhoods, your bizarre bodies,
like a joke you're both in on.

And if you're even luckier,
you'll share a strange,
joyful journey
together.

Some lovers are like the sun,
warm, nurturing hands
grabbing you
by the flowers they spawned,
pulling your best self out of your earth.
I wish you the luck of witnessing
what a skilled gardener can do to you.

But some lovers, they're like the rain—
you don't go around wishing for them,
they slip in unexpected on a summer day
and all you can do is sit quietly by a window,
admire their work,
feel your pulse slow
and your feet sink into the ground.

All you can do is realize that this,
this right there, was everything you needed,
you just didn't know to ask.

Language is born
out of lived experiences

You can hope for something extraordinary
and not yet have the vocabulary to explain it

There is so much
you can only process once
you learn to see the wide space
that sometimes separates
the comfortable and the familiar

These things I know for sure:

Time will heal all wounds
as long as you tend to them

You can't control
your way to happiness

Feelings are friends,
no matter how unbearable they can get

Growth lives on the other side of fear—
go knock on its door some time.

Living out loud
is a love letter
to send yourself every single day—

answer it.
Keep that communication flowing.

Joy lives all around you,
can't you see?
When the waves of life
force your eyes shut,
remember
the child inside knows
all it takes is practice
to see underwater.

Sometimes, feeling
like you need a change
doesn't mean you need anything
new.

Sometimes what you crave
is something old,
something loved,
something lost

waiting
to be uncovered again.

A reminder:

it's okay to want things
it's okay to want people
it's okay to state these wants
and not follow up with buts

you don't have to apologize for having desires
you don't have to wrap them in a layer of forced realism
you don't have to be made to feel
weak, or less than whole

and what does *needy* even mean?
show me the appeal of self-sufficiency,
of tanning your soft flesh into hide
whipping your suppleness into controlled form—
how is that voluntary withdrawal from connection
a worthy price to pay
for never having to risk
being let down again?

Look back and wonder:
why did you filter yourself?

If you let it,
uncertainty will make a text,
such a small thing,
also feel like everything at once.
Life or death. No safety net.

Darling, if they like you,
they'll like it no matter what:
there can't be too much of a good thing.

And if they don't,
then there was nothing left to lose.

Emotional availability is not
a switch, it is a spectrum,

it is a pool—

no matter how deep you dive, I hope
you come back up for air every once in a while.

Wild one,
if you ever decide
to civilize yourself,
please keep vestiges of yourself up.

Why would you keep on watering death
Why would you ask your abuser to heal you
Grow your own legs
and go

Grow yourself a shoulder
to lean on
and maybe a second
should you need to cry

Grow yourself two arms
to hold yourself
            loved

Breathe
life into this rebuilt body
of yours— both castle and fortress,
organic temple

Rest under your own shadow
Expand your limbs,
take space

and flourish.
Your season is beginning
right now.

If you feel
misplaced
stuck beside your body
both untethered
and an empty shell,

remember joy will always
lead you home.

acknowledgements:

Biggest thanks to you, reader. I hope this book brings you joy, I hope it makes you feel seen and heard, and I hope it serves as a map back to abundance should you ever need one.

To everyone who's ever supported my work, by buying this book or *The Sun Always Knows Where to Find Me*, or by sharing about them online or on social media: I'm so very grateful that my poems resonate with you! This bond is very special to me, and I treasure it.

Special thanks to:
Tegan, my pure ray of light, sunshine in human form, for being my biggest adventure and my number-one source of inspiration, motivation and laughter. Aurore, Flo and Lei for supporting all the chaos that fuels the creation. Will, for the new perspective and for making it make sense. Flerk, for the floof. And, as always, soy matcha lattes, peanut butter cups, Gayou, this house, my Taurus Venus, the Universe, my spirit guide. Last but not least, expert first reader Cheryl, and artist extraordinaire Julie (@juliesolvstrom), for your enthusiasm and talent.

This book is, as everything I do, a celebration of Black joy, of queer joy and of Black Women.

about the author:

Known for her raw and emotional poems, Elodie Parthenay is a storyteller based in Tiohtiá:ke (Montreal), Canada.

Harvest, her second poetry book, is a call to celebrate joy and abundance after a season of effort and planting seeds.

The first, *The Sun Always Knows Where to Find Me* (2021), a story of heartbreak and comeback to oneself, was praised for its depth and ability to mirror readers' feelings. Her work also appeared in *Woven with Brown Thread* (2021), a collection of poetry curated by Upile Chisala featuring 25 Black poets from all around the world.

Elodie studied poetry and creative writing at UCLA, where she was nominated for the Allegra Johnson Prize for Fiction for her work on an upcoming fantasy novel. A hopeless romantic and die-hard optimist, Elodie's poetry revolves about love, loss, sisterhood and self-love, as seen and experienced by a queer woman of color.

She lives with her daughter and their fluffy rescue cat, Flerken. When she's not creating poetry, she practices mindfulness meditation and writes about lifestyle, health, relationships and astrology for Women's magazines.

Find her on instagram at **@elodiewrites**, and online at **www. elodieparthenay.com**.

Printed in Great Britain
by Amazon

20778318R00089